Ride On
Bikes and Riders Who Rule

IAN PARKER

Editorial Board
David Booth • Joan Green • Jack Booth

A Harcourt Achieve Imprint

10801 N. Mopac Expressway
Building # 3
Austin, TX 78759
1.800.531.5015

Steck-Vaughn is a trademark of Harcourt Achieve Inc. registered in the
United States of America and/or other jurisdictions. All inquiries should be
mailed to Harcourt Achieve Inc., P.O. Box 27010, Austin, TX 78755.

 © 2007 Rubicon Publishing Inc.
www.rubiconpublishing.com

Associate Publisher: Miriam Bardswich
Editor: Teresa Carleton
Editorial Assistants: Caitlin Drake, Joyce Thian
Creative/Art Director: Jennifer Drew
Senior Designer: Jeanette Debusschere

Cover Image, Title Page Image–Shutterstock

7 8 9 10 11 5 4 3 2 1

Ride On: Bikes and Riders Who Rule
ISBN: 978-1-4190-4026-9

CONTENTS

CYCLING BY THE NUMBERS

2
- 2 WHEELS
- 2 PEDALS
- 2 LUNGS
- 2 LEGS

1
- 1 CHAIN
- 1 SADDLE
- 1 RIDER
- 1 PASSION

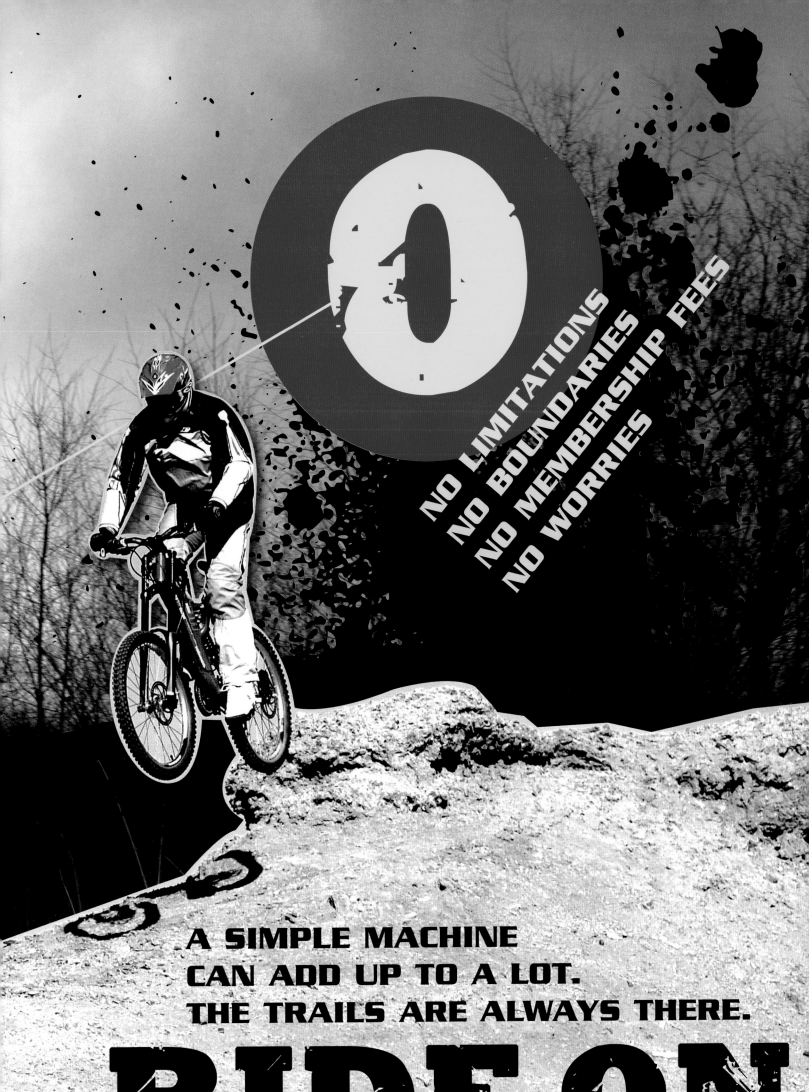

NOW YOU'RE TALKING!

A BIKING GLOSSARY

Notice that some words are *italicized* in the definitions. These words are defined somewhere else in the glossary.

BEATER
An old bike that someone would use for riding in bad weather or running errands around town

BIFF
A crash on a mountain bike

CHAIN-RING TATTOO
The dotted-line scar you get from banging your shin on the chain ring

DIGGER
A crash that results in the rider face-planting into the dirt

DRAFTING
Riders riding single file behind another rider to take advantage of the current of air (the tailwind) behind the rider in front

DRIVE TRAIN
The chain, chain rings, cogs, and pedals that allow the rider to drive the bike forward

DROPPED
When a rider can't keep up and gets left behind

GRANNY GEAR
The lowest gear available on a bike most useful for super-steep climbs

GRINDER
A long uphill climb — usually using the *granny gear*

HAMMER
To ride fast and hard

NOODLE
To ride at an easy pace

PACE LINE
A single line of riders *drafting* behind one another, taking turns leading

SUPERMAN
When a rider *biffs* and doesn't hit the ground for a long time after flying over the handlebars. This usually results in the rider taking a *digger*.

SUSPENSION
Shocks built into the front and/or rear of a bike to help absorb bumps and make the ride smoother

TABLETOP
(1) A trick where the rider launches off a jump and throws the bike sideways in midair
(2) A type of jump built so that the rider launches off a ramp, clears a flat part on top, and lands going down a ramp on the other side

TACOED
When a bike wheel gets so bent in a crash that it looks like a taco shell

TECHNICAL
A section of trail that is difficult to ride because of rocks, tree roots, drops, and other elements

TRACK STAND
A trick where the rider stops the bike and attempts to remain upright

WHEEL SUCKER
A rider who constantly drafts behind other riders and never takes a turn leading the pace line — most common in road racing

WHOOP-DE-DOOS
A series of rolling jumps all in a row

YARD SALE
A bad crash that leaves all of the rider's gear (water bottles, pump, tool bag, and so on) scattered around as if they were items at a yard sale

RIDES

warm up

How many different types of bikes can you name? Work with a partner to brainstorm different types of bikes and what they're used for.

Bikes have come a long way since the days of the early "bone shakers," and necessity is truly the mother of invention. As people wanted to go riding at faster speeds, on new and different terrain, and off bigger jumps, the bikes they rode had to become more and more specialized. Check out some of today's most popular rides for both dirt and asphalt.

MOUNTAIN BIKES

DOWNHILL

Riding downhill at breakneck speeds is what the original mountain bikes were built for. With fat tires, only a few gears, heavy-duty frame materials, and front and rear suspension with tons of travel (think BIG springs!), these rides are built to absorb the worst that a rock-strewn, super-steep downhill course can dish out. Just make sure you have a lift back up to the top — these bikes are so heavy that riding back up is tough.

travel: *amount that bike shock can be compressed (usually measured in inches)*

CHECKPOINT
Notice that each bike has both strengths and weaknesses.

FREERIDE

Freeride bikes were developed when people felt the need to do more than just rip downhill on their bikes. They have many of the same features as the downhill rides and can still absorb some pretty big hits and drops. They also have a slightly lighter frame and more gears, so they're a little easier to pedal uphill. These bikes were built for the go-anywhere, ride-anything crowd. The only drawback is that they're one of the more expensive rides to buy and maintain.

CROSS COUNTRY

Cross-country bikers still want to ride the whole mountain. With less travel in the shocks and skinnier tires, their rides are quite a bit lighter than downhill or freeride bikes. The original cross-country bikes were fully rigid, but now they generally fall into two categories: hardtail or full suspension. Hardtail rides have shocks in the front and none in the back. Full-suspension rides have shocks in the front and back. Both types will climb and tear up the flat trails faster than a freeride or downhill bike, but they won't absorb the big hits and drops as easily as the heavier bikes with bigger suspensions.

shocks: *devices on a bike that absorb vibrations*
rigid: *unable to absorb shock*

DIRT JUMPING

These bikes are usually found at dirt parks. They are made out of the heaviest, toughest materials, so they can take more abuse than just about any other bike. They have front suspension, only a few gears, and a special device that keeps the chain in place. With such heavy-duty components, you won't win any races on one of these rides!

ROAD BIKES

ROAD RACING

These are the bikes that everyone in the peloton at the Tour de France is riding. These machines are built stiff to maximize power and built light to make it easier to climb paved mountain roads. With no suspension, super-skinny wheels, and space-age frame materials, these rides are built for speed. Just stay out of the rough stuff!

peloton: *pack of bicycle racers*

TIME TRIAL

A time trial is often referred to as "the race of truth," because instead of riding in a pack, each racer must cover the course without drafting along behind anyone else. Time-trial bikes are a lot like road-racing bikes, but the shape of the frame puts the rider further forward and special handlebars are used to try to cut down on air resistance. These bikes are all about cheating the wind, but the rider needs to be careful because they can be tricky to control around tight corners.

drafting: *riding close behind another biker to take advantage of reduced wind pressure*

TRACK RACING

Track-racing bikes are built for the sole purpose of whipping around and around on a track as fast as possible. Lighter is faster, so only one gear is used and there are no brakes on these rides! The only problem is that you really wouldn't want to take this bike anywhere but on a track. (Don't worry — you probably wouldn't want to be seen on the trails in one of those skin-tight track-racing suits, anyway!)

BMX BIKES

RACING

BMX racing is all about ripping around dirt tracks as fast as possible. BMX bikes are similar to mountain bikes — only a whole lot smaller. Like mountain bikes, they have durable frames that can take a beating and wide, knobby tires to provide traction. But they also have 20-inch wheels (as opposed to the standard 26-inchers on mountain bikes) with tons of spokes to give them strength when landing jumps. These bikes tend to be lighter than the freestyle rides so that they can speed through the course as fast as possible.

FREESTYLE

These bikes were designed for one thing: tricks! Although they look a lot like racing bikes, speed is an afterthought on these rides. Freestyle bikes are equipped with pegs on the wheels so that riders have several places to put their feet while performing a trick. They also have a rotor that allows the handlebars to be spun 360 degrees without being caught up in the brake wires. Whether they're being used for bunny hops over park benches, Supermans off huge jumps, or tailtaps on the lips of half-pipes, freestyle bikes are all about riding with style.

wrap up

1. In a chart, record the main differences among mountain, road, and BMX bikes. Why are they built differently?

2. What is your favorite kind of bike riding? Work with a partner to design the perfect bike for this style of riding.

CYCLING THROUGH HISTORY

warm up

What do you think the earliest bicycles looked like? How were they different from today's bikes?

You know bikes are awesome for shredding mountains and dirt parks, and you know they're a great way to get from one place to another, but did you also know that long ago the bicycle even played a role in helping women gain equality? That's one impressive machine! From the "hobby horse" to the "bone shaker" to "bombers" and "clunkers," the history of cycling is a colorful one!

The "walking machine"

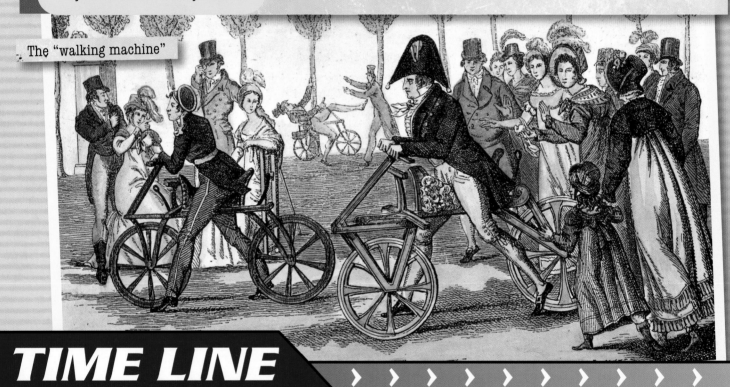

TIME LINE

› › › › › › › › › › ›

3000 B.C.E.

Mesopotamians invent the wheel.

FYI

One of the first civilizations was Mesopotamia, which means "the land between the rivers." Ancient Mesopotamia was located between the Tigris and Euphrates Rivers in what is now Iraq.

1817

Baron Von Drais invented the "walking machine." Because it didn't have pedals or a drive train, the Baron's invention wasn't much use for anything except cruising around his royal gardens, which he did by straddling the machine and pushing himself along with his feet. People thought it looked like he was riding a fake horse, so they started calling his invention the "hobby horse."

1865

Pedals were added to the hobby horse and the first two-wheeled riding machine was born. Officially known as a velocipede ("fast foot"), most people just called it the "bone shaker" because it was still made of wood with metal tires, which made for a pretty rough ride.

CHECKPOINT
Notice what made the "bone shakers" so uncomfortable to ride.

The "bone shaker"

Women could ride the new tricycle in the 1880s.

The first bicycle

1870

The first metal riding machine to be called a bicycle ("two wheels") was invented. Solid rubber tires meant a much smoother ride than the "bone shaker," but the front wheel was huge, so the bike tipped over easily.

1880

The long skirts and corsets that women wore back in the 1800s made it very difficult for them to ride these new "bicycles," so the high-wheeled tricycle ("three wheels") was invented. This rig was easier to ride, but it was much slower than a bicycle.

1890s

Metallurgy advanced to the point that cogs and chains could be produced, and suddenly bikes could have drive trains with gears. This opened up all kinds of new possibilities for the bike. They started to be mass-produced and the price came down, so more people could afford one. The first great "bicycle craze" begins!

Metallurgy: *working with metal*

1896

Common-sense clothing became acceptable for women. They could now ride two-wheeled bikes and get around just as easily as men, prompting Susan B. Anthony, the U.S. leader in the movement for women's suffrage, to remark that "the bicycle has done more for the emancipation of women than anything else in the world."

suffrage: *right to vote*
emancipation: *freedom and equal rights*

1900–1970

A period of experimentation took place during this time when people started adapting the basic structure of the bicycle to ride on different types of terrain. You want to go fast? Better make your ride lighter somehow. Want to go off-road? Better toughen up that ride somehow.

CHECKPOINT
Why was the bicycle important in helping women gain equality?

Early 1970s

A group of riders in Marin County, California, got the idea to start bombing down mountains on one-geared cruiser bikes known as "clunkers." Around the same time, a different group of riders from south of San Francisco Bay were ripping downhill on what they called "bomber" bikes. These were like the clunkers except they had ten gears and better braking systems.

Women ride bicycles — early 1940s

Riding dress

Bicycle race — 1970s

Bicycle — early 1970s

BMX race–TONY ASHBY/AFP/Getty Images; all other images–Shutterstock, istockphoto

Late 1970s

Early off-road bikes often got trashed in hardcore downhill races, so riders were forced to come up with new and stronger materials and designs. Much lighter bikes and more durable tires with knobs on them that could grip the dirt better were invented. It soon became possible to build bikes that were light enough to be ridden all over the mountain and the "mountain bike" was born.

1980s

The soaring popularity of mountain biking suddenly had competition from a new type of riding called bicycle motocross (BMX). BMX was especially popular among young people who wanted to do tricks and tear up dirt courses on two wheels.

Present

Today there are almost as many different types of bicycles as there are riders. There's a two-wheeled machine for whatever type of terrain you're into riding. Just make sure you're wearing some protective gear if you're planning to fly off any jumps on one of those old velocipedes — or you'll be giving "bone shaker" a whole new meaning!

FYI

Gary Fisher was one of the Marin County riders trying to figure out how to make bikes that were better suited for charging downhill. To this day, many people still consider him to be the grandfather of mountain biking.

Mountain bikes

Bicycle trick

BMX race

wrap up

The saying "necessity is the mother of invention" means that people invent or improve things when they need to. List examples from the time line that prove this saying is true.

WEB CONNECTIONS

Search the Web to find pictures of some of the earliest bicycles such as the "hobby horse," the "high-wheeled tricycle," and the "bone shaker." Choose one of these early bicycles, and write a paragraph describing how it is different from a modern-day bike of your choosing.

BIKING AROUND THE WORLD

CANADA
North Shore Riding

When mountain bikers started trying to ride the hilly, slick, rocky terrain on the North Shore of Vancouver, British Columbia, bridges were built over the areas that were too swampy or muddy to ride. These bridges progressed into challenging obstacles created specifically for riders to overcome.

Whitehorse, Yukon — The 24 Hours of Light

This is a cross-country race where teams compete to see who can do the most laps in 24 hours. The Yukon is referred to as "The Land of the Midnight Sun" because it gets about 22 hours of daylight in the summer time. What better place to hold a 24-hour mountain biking race?

U.S.
The Race Across America (RAAM)

RAAM is a single-stage ultra-marathon race where the starting gun fires somewhere on the West Coast (usually in California) and the finishing line is over 3,000 miles away on the other side of the continent. The racers typically ride about 22 hours per day and it takes them 7 – 10 days to finish.

Peru
Mega Avalanche

In a Mega Avalanche, everyone starts this downhill race at the same time — straight down the side of a mountain. The series started in Europe, but Peru is the leader in South America.

John F. Kennedy once said, "Nothing compares to the simple pleasure of a bike ride." It looks like people all over the world agree.

EUROPE
The Grand Tours
Each of these races sees the racers travel over 1,800 miles in about three weeks.
Tour de France
The leader wears the famous *maillot jaune* (yellow jersey).
Tour of Italy (Giro d'Italia)
The leader wears the *Maglia Rose* (pink jersey).
The Tour of Spain (Vuelta a España)
The leader wears the *Jersey de Oro* (golden jersey).

CHINA
Olympics
BMX will make its Olympic debut at the 2008 Games in Beijing. In a format similar to snowboard boardercross, four riders will start together and rip around a dirt-track obstacle course filled with jumps, bumps, and turns.

AUSTRALIA
Dirt Jam
Australia is home to some of the best BMXers in the world and the Gold Coast is where they often converge. Jam format events are favored here where winning isn't the priority, but that doesn't stop the riding from going off. As one witness recently described the Dirt Jam event that took place in Surfer's Paradise, "It was by far the most intense BMX competition of its kind ever seen in Australia, with riding that had to be seen to be believed."

SOUTH AFRICA
Riot Jam
BMX riding is spreading rapidly around the world and events in places like Durban, Cape Town, and J-Bay (Jeffreys Bay) are putting the South African BMX scene on the map! A good example is the Riot Jam series. Similar to Dirt Jam in Australia, the Riot Jams are not really contests. The riders who show up are divided into groups and are given a certain amount of time to rip up a slope-style course with multiple jumps. Judges watch the action and at the end of the day riders who have pushed their own limits are rewarded with prizes.

BMX
ADDED TO 2008 OLYMPICS

The Winter Olympics has snowboarding. Now, the Summer Games has BMX.

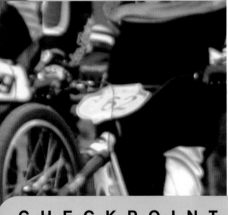

BMX racers center right—TONY ISHBY/AFP/Getty Images; all other images—Shutterstock, istockphoto

warm up

What is your favorite Olympic sport to watch on TV? Why?

CBC Sports, June 30, 2003

Bike Moto Cross, commonly known as BMX, will be added to the Olympic program at the 2008 Beijing Olympics.

One men's and one women's BMX race will replace two track cycling events, yet to be determined. The move is seen as a bid by the International Olympic Committee (IOC) to tap into a younger audience, one that watches or participates in extreme sports.

"We believe that this introduction will definitely enhance the Olympic program," said IOC president Jacques Rogge.

BMX is a TV-friendly event. Four riders on small stunt bikes start together. They negotiate a dirt-track obstacle course filled with jumps, bumps, and turns.

enhance: *improve*

CHECKPOINT
Notice how this article presents the most important facts about the story, but doesn't go into a lot of extra detail.

The fastest rider in each heat will advance in an elimination process. The heats are expected to take less than a minute each.

Rogge is an advocate of deleting sports from the Olympic program in what he calls the "gigantism" of the Games. Triathlon and tae kwon do were added to the 2000 Sydney Olympics.

The two new BMX races won't increase the number of events or athletes in Beijing, according to Rogge.

The International Cycling Union is studying which two events in the current program are the least popular, added Rogge. BMX will replace them.

advocate: *someone who works for a cause*

wrap up

Do you agree with the IOC's decision to eliminate two track cycling events to make room for BMX racing? Discuss your views about this in a small group.

TOUR DE LANCE

THE INSPIRING STORY OF LANCE ARMSTRONG

Lance Armstrong grew up in a small town called Plano, Texas. At the age of 12, his mother signed him up for a swim club that was 10 miles from his home. To get to the pool, Lance rode his bicycle there and back every day. At the age of 13, he entered his first triathlon and it wasn't long before local coaches started to notice that this young man was special. He seemed to have incredible endurance and a fierce determination that helped him win triathlons and bike races against athletes who were twice his age. After high school, Lance was named to the U.S. national cycling team and, over the next few years, he dominated several important international races. After competing in the 1992 Olympics, he turned professional. Everything seemed to be going right for the confident young American.

warm up

With a partner, jot down four or five different sports. For each sport, think of one or two athletes that were known for being among the greatest who ever played.

In the world of sports, there are a few athletes who have become so well-known that everyone knows them by their first name. These are the athletes with such remarkable skill that they take their sport to a whole new level and change our ideas about what's possible. The sport of hockey had "Wayne." Soccer had "Mia." Basketball had "Michael." Golf has "Tiger." Skateboarding has "Tony." The one name that people will always associate with the sport of cycling is "Lance."

CHECKPOINT

Notice that Lance wasn't immediately successful after turning professional.

But Lance Armstrong's career has not been without enormous challenges. In his first bike race as a professional, he finished dead last. He was over 30 minutes behind the winner and people laughed at him when he finally

THE ONE NAME THAT PEOPLE WILL ALWAYS ASSOCIATE WITH THE SPORT OF CYCLING IS SIMPLY "LANCE."

struggled to the finish line in the pouring rain. When people asked him why he didn't just give up that day, Lance responded, "My mother didn't raise a quitter." He would have to prove this again a few years later when faced with an even greater challenge, one that would threaten his life.

In 1993, at the young age of 21, Lance became the road racing world champion. That same year he got his first stage win in the Tour de France — the toughest and most famous bike race in the world. He won another stage in the 1995 Tour, but then, in 1996, came the news that would change him forever. In late September of that year, he was diagnosed with cancer. Suddenly, bicycle racing didn't matter to Lance anymore because he had to

focus all of his strength on just one thing: surviving. His doctors told him he had only a 50 percent chance of living to see his 26th birthday. People knew Lance would be lucky simply to survive, let alone get back on his bike and race again. But Lance again proved that his mother didn't raise a quitter.

Not only did Lance beat the cancer, but in 1999, he also returned to the Tour de France and emerged victorious as the overall winner. Amazingly, he was just getting started. After that first win, Lance won six more Tours and now holds the record with an incredible seven Tour de France championships. That's two more than any other rider in history.

emerged: *came out*

THE INFLUENCE THAT LANCE HAS HAD BOTH ON AND OFF HIS BIKE WILL BE REMEMBERED FOREVER.

Lance's remarkable courage and astonishing accomplishments have inspired millions of people all over the world. His Lance Armstrong Foundation (LAF), founded by Lance in 1997, has raised millions of dollars to support cancer survivors and fund research into curing this serious disease. The influence that Lance has had both on and off his bike will be remembered forever.

What follows is an excerpt from *Every Second Counts*, Lance Armstrong's 2003 follow-up book to *It's Not About the Bike*, his 2000 bestseller. In this memoir, Armstrong describes his Tour de France victories and his continuing struggle to make the most of his life — to make "every second count."

CHECKPOINT
How do you think a memoir is different from a biography?

Lance Armstrong on the Alpe d'Huez time trial 2004 Tour de France

... My friends call me Mellow Johnny. It's a play on the French term for the leader of the Tour de France, who wears a yellow jersey: the *maillot jaune*. We like to joke that Mellow Johnny is the Texan pronunciation. The name is also a play on my not-so-mellow personality. I'm Mellow Johnny, or Johnny Mellow, or, if you're feeling formal, Jonathan Mellow.

Sometimes I'm just Bike Boy. I ride my bike almost every day, even in the off-season, no matter the weather. It could be hailing, and my friends and riding partners dread the call that they know is going to come: they pick up the phone, and they hear Bike Boy on the other end, demanding, "You ridin', or you hidin'?"

One famous November day during the off-season, I rode four and a half hours through one of the strongest rainstorms on record. Seven inches of precipitation, with flash floods and road closures everywhere. I loved it. People thought I was crazy, of course. But when I'm on the bike, I feel like I'm 13 years old. I run fewer red lights now, but otherwise it's the same.

Some days, though, I feel much older than a man in his thirties; it's as if I've lived a lot longer. That's the cancer, I guess. I've spent a lot of time examining what it did to me — and the conclusion I've come to is, it didn't just change my body; it changed my mind.

I've often said cancer was the best thing that ever happened to me. But everybody wants to know what I mean by that: how could a life-threatening disease be a good thing? I say it because my illness was also my antidote: it cured me of laziness.

Before I was diagnosed, I was a slacker. I was getting paid a lot of money for a job I didn't do 100 percent, and that was more than just a shame — it was wrong. When I got sick, I told myself: if I get another chance, I'll do this right — and I'll work for something more than just myself. ...

---

dread: *fear intensely*
antidote: *remedy to work against an unwanted condition*

CHECKPOINT
Notice the distinction between body and mind that Armstrong makes here.

wrap up

1. What important personal quality did Lance learn from his mother? Discuss with a partner how this quality has helped him overcome the challenges in his life.

2. Think of another famous athlete who had to overcome a challenge or challenges before becoming successful. Write a short profile of the athlete that explains how he or she started out, what challenges he or she had to overcome, and what he or she was eventually able to accomplish.

WEB CONNECTIONS
Go online to learn more about the Lance Armstrong Foundation. Write an e-mail to a friend that describes the work that the Foundation does.

Showdown at the Shack

ILLUSTRATED BY PAUL SOEIRO

Mike Kinrade in Invermere,
British Columbia, Canada,
at a place called Paradise

QUALITY

AN INTERVIEW WITH PRO FREE

Mike Kinrade images—Courtesy Doug Le Page

TIME

RIDE MOUNTAIN BIKER MIKE KINRADE

warm up

If you had the chance to interview a professional athlete in any sport, what questions would you ask?

Top 10 finishes at "Red Bull Rampage," "Most Notable Section in a Bike Movie Segment," Bike Video Poll Awards "Best Air" nomination, regular appearances on action sports TV shows, competing in the international Slopestyle Invitational series ... All of these accomplishments are indications of a mountain biker who has taken his riding to the top level. All of these accomplishments (and more!) also appear on the résumé of pro freerider Mike Kinrade. Being a professional mountain bike rider definitely has some challenges, but to Mike it's really all about "spending some quality time with my big bike and seeing what we can find together."

29

Mike Kinrade, Invermere,
British Columbia

BP: *How did you first get into mountain biking?*

MK: I grew up in Nelson, British Columbia, Canada. It's a town that is extremely supportive of outdoor activities and has so much mountain biking in it and the surrounding area that it basically breeds high-caliber riders with each passing generation. I discovered mountain biking by going out on the trails every day with my friends and through the years we started to revolve our lives around it. We got into building bigger airs, going faster down the trails, and then started filming it. We didn't think that people outside of Nelson would recognize us but eventually we gained a reputation and made a living out of it.

CHECKPOINT
Notice how Mike started out mountain biking and then gradually progressed to being a professional rider.

BP: *How would you describe the type of riding that you do the most?*

MK: All out! I like to go for the lines that bring me into the mountains and allow me to explore just how big I can go with my bike. My favorite time riding is exploring new terrain in British Columbia (and the rest of the world) and seeing how I can push myself.

MK: Being a professional mountain biker. I ride at the highest level in a sport that just about everyone has tried. I'm pretty stoked on that. But honestly, there's no better feeling than flying through the air on a mountain bike. Just your own legs sailing you and your bike off some huge air.

BP: *What are some of the biggest challenges of being a pro rider?*

MK: Sometimes it feels like a lot of work. I'll get stressed out when I have a lot of things on my plate to finish. If I'm not on my bike, I'm not that happy of a guy. I also don't like working on my bike when it needs tuning or fixing; it takes me too long. But the guys at the shop won't work on it for me. Even if I pay them, they make me work on it. I'm supposed to know how to fix everything on my bike, and now I do ... I can do it all very slowly.

BP: *How did you make the transition to being a pro rider?*

MK: When I was about 18, I helped make a film called *Hidden Pleasures* that pushed me to ride harder and perform better for the camera. A little bit of "Kodak Courage" never hurt anyone! When I was still a teenager, I was invited to events like the "Red Bull Rampage" and placed high. From there, I just grew in my abilities and the exposure which I was getting in the media. Back in 2004, I was signed by Devinci Cycles as an employee of theirs whose job it is to ride and promote the brand.

BP: *What's a typical riding day like for you?*

MK: Typically, I like to start early when the day is fresh and I have a lot of time to ride, eat, ride, then eat, then ride, followed by eating. After it's all done, I'll go to the gym and do some stretching and conditioning. I'll usually spend a good part of my riding time in front of the lens of a photographer or cinematographer. In between, I manage the business side of being a pro athlete and exploring and building new stunts, jumps, or trails to shoot on.

BP: *What's the most rewarding thing about being a professional mountain biker?*

cinematographer: *person who films movies*

wrap up

1. What personal qualities do you think Mike has that have allowed him to become so successful? Explain your answer.

2. Based on Mike's comments and your own ideas, make a comparison chart that lists the pros (good things) and cons (not so good things) about being a professional mountain biker. Compare your chart to a partner's and add any new ideas to your list.

WEB CONNECTIONS

Go to Mike Kinrade's Web site **http://www.kinradical.com**. Check out some of the competitions on his résumé. Go online to find out more about one of these competitions and create a poster advertising it.

HAMMER TIME

warm up

Have you ever been nervous before participating in some kind of competition? Work with a partner to list things a person can do to help stay calm.

Eyes closed.

"Riders ready …"

Breathe.

"3"

Stand up on the pedals …

"2"

Load up the power leg …

"1"

Let the gate drop …

"Go"

EXPLODE! Hammer! Hammer! Hammer!

First hit … stay low … flex the legs ...

Absorb the landing …

Hammer!

High on the bank …

Compress out of the turn …

Burst out of it … watch the next rider …

Rock the bars, make space ...

Don't let him in …

Hammer!

C H E C K P O I N T

Notice that the shape this poem makes resembles a rolling, up-and-down bike course.

Hammer: *ride fast and hard*

32

BMX racer top left–Robert Laberge/Getty Images for USOC; all other images–Shutterstock,istockphoto

Flex and stay low …

Get ready to suck up the rollers …

Carry the speed … 1 … 2 … 3 … gap the last one …

Absorb the landing …

Relaxed arms …

Hammer!

Now the table top …

Stay square on the approach …

Suck up the lip … stay flexed in the air …

Absorb the landing.

Finish …

Hold your line …

Everything you've got now … empty the tank …

Hammer! Hammer! Hammer! Hammer! Hammer! Hammer!

Loudspeaker …

"3rd call. Race #14 at Summerslam Jam.

All Riders to the start please …"

"Yo, Raymond. Get up! That's us, bro."

Eyes open.

Make it happen.

wrap up

1. List several words and phrases that the poet uses to convey a sense of urgency and tension in the poem.

2. Choose an activity that you like to do and create your own shape poem about it.

suck up the rollers: *use your legs to try to keep wheels on the ground when going over rolling bumps*
gap: *jump over*

RACING THE MEGA AVALANCHE IN PERU

warm up

By Katrina Strand

If you could go mountain biking anywhere in the world, where would you choose and why? Explain your answer to a partner.

My bike is my adventure buddy. We are always on a mission to travel to cool places and meet cool people. Sometimes it's a hop and a skip away to the North Shore, but most recently, he (yes, he) brought me to Peru to explore and race a Mega Avalanche. …

After much organizing, several riders met up in the Andes — there were Europeans, South Americans, and we two Canadian girls. We played tourist for the first few days and were awed by some surreal Inca sights. …

Then it was time to ride.

surreal: *fantastic*

CHECKPOINT
As you read, notice how mountain bikers have developed their own short form for certain words (like "downhill" and "cross country").

In case you haven't heard of a Mega Avalanche, they're mass-start enduro DH races that cover anywhere between 15 and 25 kilometers [9 and 12 miles] — straight down the side of a mountain. The series started in Europe and is now going international. Riders are lined up according to seeding times and then it's game on. Everyone hustles down the course together — girls, guys, pro, amateur, young, and old. And you do this twice.

seeding: *in the order of competition*

Racers break away from the start line of the 2005 Mega Avalanche mountain bike race in Peru. The mass-start downhill is unique in mountain biking.

Katrina Strand and Claire Buchar take a self-portrait while sightseeing in Peru.

35

People are stoked on the non-traditional race format because it tends to attract a lot of recreational riders. You can race the whole race with a buddy if you want. There are pros that do the series and are extremely serious, but for the most part everyone is there to ride and have fun with their friends. I'm hoping that the series will push its way into North America some time soon. It would take off.

Mega Avalanche courses typically combine DH and XC, and the best times are usually over an hour. Normally, riders will ride the lightest bike possible that is still capable of pinning it downhill when necessary but likes to climb as well.

CHECKPOINT

Notice the type of bicycle required.

I was a little nervous 'cause my bike is more DH than XC, but it turned out that this course was mostly downhill and quite a bit shorter than usual. No one complained about the lack of peddling — mostly down was a good thing when racing at an elevation of 4,300 m [14,100 ft.]. In case you hadn't figured it out, this is high! Everything that takes energy is difficult, and the little push to the top of the course required a snack break. ...

stoked: *excited about*

My partner in crime (that would be Claire Buchar) and I prepared ourselves for race day. This is the only DH race you need to race with a backpack full of water, food, change of clothes, and everything for changing a flat. A little aspirin and some special tea before the ascent helped thin out our blood and make the altitude more tolerable, and we were ready to race.

The ladies were in line B, right behind the fastest seeding times from the day before. Riders like World Cup DH racers Cedric Gracia, Markolf Berchtold, Gee Atherton, and Diana McGrath, DH World Champion Fabien Barel, Olympic XC winner Miguel Martinez, and Mega Avalanche series winner René Wildhaber were all ready to battle. ...

There were only four girls in the race but that didn't take away from the avalanche experience — that's for sure! There were a lot of sketchy passes at the top and a few stops to check up on the random casualty. For the most part, Claire and I cruised in unison and (coincidentally!) tied the first race. What a pleasant surprise! ...

casualty: *accident; injury*
unison: *together; at the same time*

Katrina Strand rails a berm on the El Prado downhill track in the Pachacamac region, near Lima, Peru.

During the second run, I rode over the finish line alone, taking first, while Claire stood on the sidelines with a flat. She still pulled off a second place, though, because of the points she accumulated with the first run. Crazy Caroll, the local Peruvian ripper, finished third. Unfortunately, Diana McGrath had a bad crash in the first race and didn't make it to the second one. I was bummed about that and have been sending her quick healing thoughts ever since.

The men charged hard and in the end, René Wildhaber won both races; his fastest time was 22:59. Cedric Gracia took second and Gee Atherton was third. They all looked a little green after the race, so I'm assuming it was pedal to the metal the whole way down for the boys. ...

Claire Buchar (front) and Katrina Strand ride the proposed 2006 Mega Avalanche course. On the first day, before practice for the 2005 event started, the riders were given a preview of the track.

CHECKPOINT

Why would they be "green"? What connection does "pedal to the metal" have with being green?

Peru is an unbelievable country and my time there definitely won't be forgotten! The mountains, the people, the history, and the culture are fascinating. ... Everything about it is intense, so be prepared for any situation, 'cause anything goes. It is a place for the adventurous. And, of course, don't forget your bike! ...

wrap up

1. Choose three highlights of the race, and describe these in your own words.

2. Create a travel brochure to advertise a great mountain biking destination. You can choose anywhere in the world. Remember to include details such as why it's a great place to mountain bike, how to get there, what accommodations are available, how much it costs, and any other information that would be important for travelers to know.

WEB CONNECTIONS

Type the words Mega Avalanche into a search engine to get a fuller description of this type of racing and other destinations around the world where it occurs. Make up a fact sheet with the information that you find.

HOW TO DO A WHEELIE

warm up

Think of a skill that you know how to do well (it could be any skill at all — anything from making pancakes to throwing a Frisbee!). Describe to a partner how to do this skill. Make sure you provide all the important details.

The "wheelie" in cycling is like the "ollie" in skateboarding: it's the most well-known trick and it's the first step when performing other, more advanced tricks.

STEP 1

THE SETUP

Get your bike into a pretty low gear. While rolling slowly forward, level your pedals with the ground with your stronger foot in front. (If your crank were a clock, your pedals would be at 3 and 9 o'clock.) Hold your handlebars with your arms slightly bent. Sit toward the back of your seat.

STEP 2

THE PEDAL KICK

A pedal kick is a really short, hard stroke of the pedal. This is how you get a wheelie started and is also a great technique for popping your front wheel over roots, rocks, curbs, and any other small obstacles that get in your path. To do it, back pedal your front foot a bit from the 3 o'clock position to about 2 o'clock, and then drive it quickly forward one quarter of a turn to about 6 o'clock. As you drive your foot forward, yank up on the handlebars. This will raise your front wheel off the ground.

STEP 3

WHEELIE TIME

Once your front wheel is off the ground, straighten your arms and pedal slowly — don't stop! To keep your wheel up, you have to keep pedaling steadily. If you feel like you're going to fall backward (this happens sometimes — make sure you have your helmet on!), just lightly squeeze your rear brake. This will automatically drop your front wheel back to the ground.

TIPS

Wheelies take practice, so give yourself lots of time to learn this trick. Get your pedal kick dialed in and work on getting your front wheel off the ground. Then you can start doing a few pedal strokes while the wheel is up. Gradually increase the length of your wheelies until you can make it all the way to your friend's place to let him or her know it's time to go riding!

wrap up

1. What do you think is the most difficult part of this activity? Discuss with a partner.

2. Think of a skill that you know how to do well (it could be the same one from the Warm Up activity or a different one). Write out instructions on how to perform this skill. Try to keep the instructions clear without being too long.

WEB CONNECTIONS

Search the Web to find a list of instructions on how to do an activity that you would like to know how to do. Read the instructions carefully, jot down the main ideas, and then explain to a partner how to do the activity.

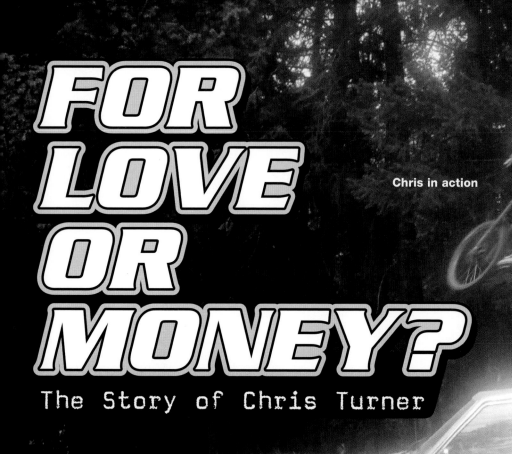

FOR LOVE OR MONEY?

The Story of Chris Turner

Chris in action

warm up

What are some of the reasons that people participate in mountain biking? Work with a partner to list as many reasons as possible.

Professional mountain bikers get paid to go out riding almost every day. They get free bikes, clothing, and other gear. They travel around the world to compete in front of adoring fans. It's true that pro riders seem to have a pretty good life, and that's why a lot of young riders dream of getting sponsored and making a living at what they love to do. But the truth is, for every pro rider throwing down at big competitions and getting free stuff, there are probably ten thousand other mountain bikers tearing up the trails who aren't getting paid to do it. For these

riders, mountain biking might not be how they make their living, but it's an important part of how they choose to live their lives. Chris Turner was one of these riders.

CHECKPOINT

Note some differences between a "professional" mountain biker and an "amateur" one.

"CT" loved mountain biking, and he was good at it. His friends will tell you stories of how he always seemed to find the sickest lines and stomp the biggest drops with a fluid style that was all his own. Growing up near the North Shore of Vancouver, British Columbia, Canada and its world- famous freeride mountain biking terrain, he took every chance he could to develop his skills. Many who knew Chris thought

fluid: *smooth and effortless*

he should enter some competitions and try to get sponsored — they were sure he was good enough to become a professional mountain biker. But for "CT," mountain biking wasn't just about pedaling a bike and it certainly wasn't about trying to make money while doing it. Chris loved mountain biking because he loved being outside. He loved riding with his friends and pushing each other to go bigger and ride more challenging terrain. He loved mountain biking because it gave him a way to express himself — flowing the smooth and fast terrain when he was just chilling with his friends, hitting the more technical lines and the steeper drops when he was feeling more aggressive. In a way, Chris loved mountain biking because it reflected the things he really valued in his life like friendship, creative expression, and a love of the outdoors. It was the same approach he brought to all the other sports he loved and excelled at like snowboarding, surfing, and soccer.

Professional mountain bikers are amazing athletes who constantly push the sport to new levels and often put themselves at risk of injury in order to stay competitive and

represent their sponsors. In some ways, it's too bad more young rippers can't get paid to ride their bikes. But for the hundreds of thousands of amateur riders like Chris Turner, hopping on their bikes and heading out to the trails with friends on any given day, mountain biking represents a way of life that they choose to live because they love it. You couldn't even pay them to stop!

Sadly, Chris "CT" Turner passed away suddenly in the spring of 2005.

---

flowing: *riding smoothly and rhythmically*

wrap up

1. In your own words, explain how Chris used mountain biking to express himself.

2. Why do you think the title of this article is "For Love or Money"? Do you think all pro mountain bikers only ride for the money? Why or why not? Explain your answer to a partner.

WEB CONNECTIONS

Go online to find out more about the North Shore mountain biking scene. Write an e-mail to a friend that describes why this mountain biking area is so special.

The King of the Canyon

warm up

Have you ever had to overcome a tough challenge in a sport or activity that you participate in? Tell a partner what the challenge was and whether you overcame it or not.

Devon lay still and mentally scanned his body for signs of injury. No blood? Check. No broken bones sticking out? Check. His next task was to try to sort out the soft flesh of his limbs from the hard aluminum and rubber of his mountain bike and the thorny branches of the tree they were both wrapped around. "Owww," he groaned weakly. The next words he heard were from his best friend, Ray, as he rode back toward the spot where Devon and his bike were piled in a heap on the side of the trail.

"Dude, are you all right?" Ray asked anxiously.

The only response was another miserable "Owww" from the pile of bike, tree, and limbs.

"Now you know why they call it the Boneyard," offered Ray. "Gnarly," he summarized.

C H E C K P O I N T
Why is the Boneyard such a difficult section of trail to ride?

Devon awkwardly untangled himself. He already knew why they called this section of trail the Boneyard. If the maze of exposed tree roots and sharp rocks didn't separate you from your bike, the steep descents and patches of loose sand would get you. At least they always got Devon. He had been trying for months to ride this section of trail without crashing but so far it had always got the better of him. Ray, on the other hand, always rode the Boneyard flawlessly, hardly breaking a sweat.

"Don't worry, Dev. You'll get it for the King of the Canyon tomorrow."

Devon didn't share his friend's confidence. The King of the Canyon was the biggest event on the local racing calendar. It always took place toward the end of the mountain biking season when the leaves had started to

flawlessly: *without a mistake*

If the maze of exposed tree roots and sharp rocks didn't separate you from your bike, the steep descents and patches of loose sand would get you.

change. The course covered 30 miles of the most scenic single-track trails in the Grey Mountain area — including the Boneyard. Devon had been hitting the trails almost every day all summer and his riding had improved steadily. He even placed in the top ten in two races. Secretly, Devon's goal all year had been to crack the top five in the King of the Canyon race, but to do this, he would have to ride the Boneyard without ending up in a bike pretzel.

As the boys rode home in silence, his goal seemed further out of reach than ever.

The next morning, Devon awoke feeling slightly more upbeat. The sunshine pouring through his bedroom window told him it would be a superb fall day. "At the very least," he reassured himself, "it will be a beautiful ride." He tried to ignore his next thought, "Even if I end up admiring this blue sky lying flat on my back tangled up in a tree in the Boneyard."

As the riders gathered at the start line, Devon found a position about three rows behind the big "King of the Canyon" banner. From the front row, Ray caught Devon's eye and flashed a thumbs-up. "Tear it up, bro!" he called. Devon had to smile.

"Have a good ride, Ray," he replied.

Waiting for the starting horn, Devon glanced around nervously at the other riders. He was barely listening while the race director called out the final instructions and mentioned something about "the code of the trail." He tried his best to stay calm. "Breathe," he told himself. "You can do this." The loud blast of the starting horn ripped through his thoughts.

MILE ZERO

The pack rolled slowly for just a few seconds while shoes clipped into pedals with a clatter. Then the opening sprint was on. In a cross-country race, all the top riders try to be the first to cover the distance between the wide starting area and the first single-track section because it's much harder to make passes once everyone is riding single file. Devon had never been a great sprinter. He was in 16th place at the start of the single-track. "I've got some work to do," he told himself.

MILE 16

The first half of the course was mostly a long and brutal climb up the narrow trails of Grey Mountain. Devon was a good climber and was gradually overtaking some of the riders ahead of him who had started too fast. He had moved up to 11th place.

MILE 21

The course reached its highest point where Grey Mountain Road met the downhill trail called "Easy Money," which was one of Devon's favorites. "Now the fun starts," he told himself. He was breathing hard. His efforts were paying off — he was riding well and now found himself in eighth place.

MILE 25

With each passing mile, Devon's confidence grew. He rode the Easy Money section swiftly and fluidly. He suddenly realized with surprise that not only was he having a great race, he was also having fun. He even let himself smile a few times. By the time he got to the Boneyard, he was in fifth place, right on Aaron Iceton's back wheel. "No smiles now," he told himself. "Time to focus."

He suddenly realized with surprise that not only was he having a great race, he was also having fun.

CHECKPOINT
Do you think Devon will finish in the top five?

Devon took his riding to a whole new level in the Boneyard that day. He navigated the roots and rocks smoothly. He swooped down the descents faster than he ever had before. His riding suddenly had a flow and a rhythm to it.

At the final curve of one especially steep descent, Devon blew past Aaron. He was now in fourth place with just a couple of miles of flat-riding to go until the finish. The thought of finishing in the top five and achieving his goal filled him with excitement, but it was then that a thunderous sound behind him ripped through the still air. What he heard was the all-too-familiar crash of aluminum scraping against tree and rock, followed by a painful shriek. For a split second, a voice in Devon's head told him to keep pedaling — toward the finish line, toward his goal,

but then a louder voice commanded him to stop. He squeezed his brakes, dismounted, and ran back to where Aaron and his bike lay in a tangled heap.

The sixth-place rider blew by and Devon could see two more riders bombing toward them.

Devon could see that Aaron was holding his shoulder and bleeding from a gash on his elbow. "Hey, are you good?" he called. The response he got was not what he expected.

"Dude, what are you doing? I'll be OK. You're riding awesome — keep going!"

Devon hesitated. "What about your arm?"

"I'm fine — get outta here!" Aaron practically screamed at him.

He squeezed his brakes, dismounted, and ran back to where Aaron and his bike lay in a tangled heap.

By the time he got back on his bike, Devon had dropped back to seventh place. He rode strongly over the last few miles, but it wasn't enough. As he rolled under the finishing banner, he was met by Ray, who had finished second and was upbeat as always. "Yeah, Dev! Great ride, bro!"

As Devon slowly rode home, he was surprised that he, too, was feeling pretty upbeat. A small part of him felt disappointed at not achieving his goal, but a bigger part of him felt proud and satisfied. After all, he did have a great ride. He even conquered the Boneyard.

Lost in thought, Devon didn't realize Aaron had ridden up behind him. He was riding with one hand on the handlebars because the other was in a sling.

"Hey," he called. "You had fourth place sewn up, dude."

Devon noted the bloodied bandage on his elbow. "You all right?" he asked.

"Bah," Aaron dismissed him. "This is nothing. Listen," he continued. "Thanks for stopping. I guess you take that 'code of the trail' stuff seriously, huh?"

Devon glanced back at him. The code of the trail calls on mountain bikers to look out for each other out on the trails — no matter what's at stake. Devon then realized he had another reason to feel proud of himself that day.

CHECKPOINT
Notice how Devon feels about his race.

"Nah," he responded casually. "I was just checking to see if I could steal something from you while you were all tangled up in your bike."

Aaron laughed out loud. "Hey," he continued. "You want to go riding tomorrow?"

Devon then realized he had another reason to feel proud of himself that day.

FYI

The "King of the Canyon" is a real race that takes place each September in Whitehorse, Yukon, Canada.

wrap up

1. Create a time line for the "King of the Canyon" race. Include specific events from the story and add other events that could have happened, such as details about Ray's race.

2. Write an alternate ending for the story starting at Mile 25.

WEB CONNECTIONS

Use the Web to find the results of a recent bike

ACKNOWLEDGMENTS

The publisher gratefully acknowledges the following for permission to reprint copyrighted material in this book.

Every reasonable effort has been made to trace the owners of copyrighted material and to make due acknowledgment. Any errors or omissions drawn to our attention will be gladly rectified in future editions.

CBC Sports: "BMX added to 2008 Olympics" from CBC Sports. Available online at http://www.cbc.ca/story/sports/national/2003/06/30/Sports/bmx030630.html

Katrina Strand: "Racing the Mega Avalanche in Peru," by Katrina Strand. Permission courtesy of Katrina Strand and nsmb.com. Available online at http://www.nsmb.com/trail_tales/mega_peru_03_05.php

Lance Armstrong and Sally Jenkins: *Every Second Counts,* by Lance Armstrong and Sally Jenkins. New York: Broadway Books, 2003.